GREAT
AFRICAN-
AMERICAN
LAWYERS

Other titles in the *Collective Biographies* Series

—Collective Biographies—

GREAT AFRICAN-AMERICAN LAWYERS

Raising the Bar of Freedom

Carole Boston Weatherford

Enslow Publishers, Inc.

40 Industrial Road   PO Box 38
Box 398   Aldershot
Berkeley Heights, NJ 07922   Hants GU12 6BP
USA   UK

http://www.enslow.com

Library of Congress Cataloging-in-Publication Data

Weatherford, Carole Boston, 1956–
    Great African-American lawyers: raising the bar of freedom / Carole Boston
Weatherford.
        p. cm.— (Collective biographies)
Includes bibliographical references and index.
Summary: Ten biographies of African American lawyers, including Charles
Hamilton Houston, William Henry Hastie, Thurgood Marshall, Constance
Baker Motley, Benjamin Hooks, Douglas Wilder, Barbara Jordan,
Johnnie Cochran, Marian Wright Edelman, and Carol Moseley-Braun.
    ISBN 0-7660-1837-7
    1. African American lawyers—Biography—Juvenile literature. [1.
Lawyers. 2. African Americans—Biography.] I. Title. II. Series.
    KF372 .W43 2002
    340'.092'2—dc21

                            2001006704

Printed in the United States of America

10 9 8 7 6 5 4 3 2 1

To Our Readers:
We have done our best to make sure all Internet addresses in this book were active and
appropriate when we went to press. However, the author and the publisher have no
control over and assume no liability for the material available on those Internet sites
or on other Web sites they may link to. Any comments or suggestions can be sent by
e-mail to comments@enslow.com or to the address on the back cover.

Every effort has been made to locate all copyright holders of material used in this
book. If any errors or omissions have occurred, corrections will be made in future
editions of this book.

Illustration Credits: The Barbara Jordan Archives, Texas Southern
University, pp. 66, 72; Library of Congress, pp. 16, 20, 27, 30, 40;
Moorland Spingarn Research Center, p. 10; National Archives, p. 36; The
Star Ledger/photo by Andrew Mills, p. 76; The Star Ledger/photo by
Jennifer Hulshizer, p. 58; The Star Ledger/photo by Joe Gigli, p. 62; The
Star Ledger/photo by Mark Abraham, pp. 90, 94, 100; The Star
Ledger/photo by Noah Addis, p. 81; The Star Ledger/photo by Rich Krauss,
p. 84; The Star Ledger/photo by Robert Eberle, pp. 48, 53; United States
District Court, Southern District of New York/photo by Chester Higgins,
Jr., p. 45.

Cover Illustrations: The Barbara Jordan Archives, Texas Southern University,
bottom left; Library of Congress, top left; The Star Ledger/photo by Andrew
Mills, bottom right; The Star Ledger/photo by Rich Krauss, top right.

Contents

Introduction

In the nineteenth century, African-American lawyers had to settle for small victories. During slavery and Reconstruction, black lawyers' greatest accomplishment was merely overcoming racial barriers to enter the legal profession.

In 1844 businessman Macon Allen applied for a license to practice law in Maine. The court rejected him, claiming he was not a citizen. A year later he passed a tough examination and was admitted to the bar. Allen became the first licensed African-American lawyer in the United States. He set up practice in Boston, Massachusetts, and became justice of the peace. He later moved to the South to help the region's large population of freed slaves. In South Carolina, he became a municipal judge—one of the first blacks to sit on the bench in the United States.

In 1865, the year the Civil War ended, John Rock became the first African-American lawyer admitted to practice before the U.S. Supreme Court. In 1870, Jonathan Jasper Wright, formerly a legal adviser to the Freedmen's Bureau, was elected a South Carolina State Supreme Court justice. He was the first African American to hold a major judgeship.

Charlotte Ray, a Howard University law school graduate, was admitted to practice law in Washington, D.C., in 1872. She was the first African-American female attorney in the United States.

In the 1896 *Plessy* v. *Ferguson* case, the U.S. Supreme Court ruled that segregation was constitutional as long as facilities for blacks and whites were "separate but equal." This court ruling legalized segregation and led to the passage of so-called Jim Crow laws. These laws denied blacks the right to vote and allowed discrimination in education, employment, housing, and the use of public facilities and transportation.

By 1900 there were more than seven hundred African-American lawyers in the United States. From those ranks came the lawyers who waged the legal struggle for racial equality: Charles Hamilton Houston, the struggle's chief legal strategist; Thurgood Marshall, the first African American appointed as a U.S. Supreme Court justice; and William Henry Hastie, the first African American to serve on the federal bench.

These legal pioneers inspired a generation of black attorneys who continued the freedom struggle. They scored their own firsts in law and politics. Some of the lawyers profiled in this book, like Constance Baker Motley, Marian Wright Edelman, and Benjamin Lawson Hooks, distinguished themselves on the civil rights front.

Other African-American lawyers, like Barbara Jordan, L. Douglas Wilder, and Carol Moseley-Braun, blazed trails in politics. Johnnie Cochran's career took a different route, however. He is best known as a trial attorney for celebrity clients.

Whether working in courtrooms or capitols, these brilliant African-American lawyers shared a commitment to professional achievement and social justice. They argued cases and advanced causes that altered history. Both yesterday and today, they continue to tear down racial barriers in American society.

Charles Hamilton Houston

Charles Hamilton Houston

(1895–1950)

Charles Hamilton Houston hailed from a long line of rebels and intellectuals. His paternal grandparents both fled slavery. His grandfather, Thomas Jefferson Houston, became a conductor on the Underground Railroad and a Baptist minister.

By 1891 the Houston family had moved to Washington, D.C. There, the Houstons' oldest son, William, attended Howard University's evening law department. William soon married Mary Ethel Hamilton, a teacher he met in Paducah, Kentucky.

Charles Hamilton Houston was born September 3, 1895, in Washington, D.C., the only child of William and Mary Houston. William Houston, an attorney, had a law practice and also worked for the federal government. Mary Houston, a former schoolteacher, was a hairdresser and seamstress for the wives of important lawmakers and government officials.

William and Mary Houston valued education and instilled in their son a love of books. Nicknamed Charlie, he was known as a bookworm. He played outdoor sports but sometimes preferred practicing the piano, visiting the zoo, and attending concerts.

From first through eighth grade, Charlie attended Garrison Elementary, a segregated Washington, D.C., public school. He went on to M Street High School, the nation's first and best college preparatory high school for African Americans. In 1911, at age fifteen, he graduated as valedictorian from M Street High School.

That same year Charles entered Amherst College in Massachusetts. He was the only African-American student in his class. Charles was elected to Phi Beta Kappa, a national honor society, and graduated with highest honors in 1915. At commencement, his valedictory address focused on African-American poet Paul Laurence Dunbar.

Just nineteen years old, Charles dreamed of being a concert pianist. William Houston arranged for Charles to fill a temporary post as English instructor at Howard University.

When the United States entered World War I, Charles Houston and other draft-age Howard men pressed Congress and the War Department for an officers' training camp for African Americans.

Military experience brought Houston's career goals into focus. He was an army judge advocate in a few cases at Camp Meade, Maryland. His duties were to investigate and prosecute offenses by army soldiers. He saw the army unfairly punish African-American soldiers.

In France with the American Expeditionary Forces, African-American officers, like Houston, endured segregated policies, unfair performance evaluations, and attacks by white officers. "I made up my mind that I would never get caught again without knowing my rights," he recalled, "that if luck was with me, and I got through this war, I would study law and use my time fighting for men who could not strike back."[1]

When he returned home to the United States, Houston found racial turmoil. In 1919 race riots erupted in Washington, D.C., and other cities. This violence strengthened Houston's resolve to become a lawyer.

In September 1919, Houston entered Harvard Law School. Despite the challenging course work, Houston joined the all-black Alpha Phi Alpha fraternity and organized a law club for Jewish and African-American students. At Harvard he became the first African-American editor of the *Harvard Law Review*. In 1922 he graduated in the top 5 percent of his class with a bachelor of laws degree.

With an aim to teach future African-American lawyers, he won a scholarship to continue his legal studies. The next year he became the first African American to receive a doctoral degree in juridical science (an advanced degree in the study of law) from Harvard. In 1923 he won a travel fellowship and went to the University of Madrid to study civil law.

A year later he returned to Washington, D.C., and married Margaret Maron. After passing the bar examination, he joined his father's downtown law firm, renamed Houston & Houston. The younger Houston also began teaching in Howard University's evening law department.

Howard University School of Law, the first black law school in the United States, opened in 1869. By 1924 the school had produced more than three fourths of the nation's practicing black attorneys.[2] However, the university faced pressure from the American Association of Law Schools (AALS) and the American Bar Association (ABA) to raise academic standards and close the part-time evening law department. The AALS and ABA both acted as accrediting agencies for law schools. Because graduates of unaccredited law schools could not take the bar exam required to become licensed attorneys, Howard University moved to improve its curriculum and admissions policies.

In 1929, Houston was named vice dean of Howard Law School. Houston closed the evening law program, raised admissions standards, and improved the faculty, library, and curriculum. In 1930 the law school became accredited.

Houston then embarked on a broader mission. "[The] Negro lawyer," he said, "must be trained as social engineer and group interpreter. Due to the Negro's social and political condition . . . the Negro lawyer must be prepared to anticipate, guide and interpret his advancement."[3]

At Howard, Houston aimed to train an army of African-American lawyers to battle for racial equality. He added courses in civil rights law. He encouraged students to return to their communities and challenge discrimination in the courts. "He made it clear to all of us that when we were done, we were expected to go out and do something with our lives," former student and future Supreme Court Justice Thurgood Marshall recalled.[4]

Houston also did his civic duty. From 1933 to 1935 he served on the District of Columbia Board of Education.

In 1935 the National Association for the Advancement of Colored People (NAACP), America's oldest and largest civil rights group, enlisted Houston as its first full-time, paid special counsel. He led a legal action campaign against the separate but equal doctrine that had been established by the U.S. Supreme Court decision in the 1896 *Plessy* v. *Ferguson* case.

In a 1935 article, Houston wrote: ". . . The ultimate objective . . . is [to end] . . . segregation in public education, whether in the admission

Charles Hamilton Houston (center) is credited with helping Howard University Law School gain accreditation and challenge segregation. He appears here with other NAACP Legal Defense Lawyers.

of activities of students, the appointment or advancement of teachers, or administrative control."[5]

Thurgood Marshall sought the NAACP's help in representing Donald Murray, an African-American man barred from the all-white University of Maryland Law School. Houston helped Marshall argue the case. The Maryland Court of Appeals ordered the university's law school to admit African

Americans.[6] That was Marshall's first big case and Houston's first victory as NAACP special counsel.

Houston had many duties as special counsel: filing lawsuits, arguing cases, and delivering speeches to raise funds and rally public support for the NAACP's legal campaign. In addition, he was responsible for other NAACP legal work. To meet these demands, he recruited Marshall as assistant special counsel.

Houston's next courtroom victory was in *Missouri ex rel Gaines* v. *Canada.* The University of Missouri Law School would not admit Lloyd Gaines, an African-American man, to its all-white law school. Instead it offered him a scholarship to an out-of-state law school. The U.S. Supreme Court ruled that scholarships to out-of-state graduate schools do not constitute equal educational opportunities.[7]

Under Houston's leadership, the NAACP tackled the death penalty, employment and housing discrimination cases, and challenged all-white labor unions and all-white juries. Also, the NAACP lawyers investigated discrimination in public transportation and fought successfully in some states for the equalization of teacher salaries.[8]

In 1937, Charles and Margaret Houston divorced. That same year, Houston married Henrietta Williams. They had one son.

Houston moved his office to Washington, D.C., in 1938 and returned to the law firm with his father and close friend William Henry Hastie. Houston resigned his position as special counsel to the NAACP two years later. As special counsel, he had laid the groundwork for *Brown* v. *Board of Education*, the landmark 1954 school desegregation case.

Houston remained on the NAACP National Legal Committee and continued to advocate for civil rights. As general counsel for the International Association of Railway Employees and the Association of Colored Railway Trainmen and Locomotive Firemen, he argued against discriminatory labor practices.

Houston also began the fight to desegregate Washington, D.C., public schools. In 1944, President Harry Truman appointed Houston to the Fair Labor Practices Committee. Houston resigned a year later to protest Truman's refusal to ban discrimination by the Washington Capital Transit Authority.[9]

Houston dedicated his career to the cause of desegregation. His columns on racial and international issues regularly appeared in the *Baltimore Afro-American* newspaper. He cofounded the all-black Washington Bar Association because blacks were banned from the District of Columbia Bar Association.

In 1947, Fisk University, a black institution in Nashville, Tennessee, awarded Houston an honorary doctor of laws degree.

Houston died April 22, 1950, of a heart attack. He was posthumously awarded the NAACP Spingarn Medal, the organization's highest honor.

Federal Judge William Henry Hastie, Houston's colleague and close friend, wrote in 1950 that Houston "led us through the legal wilderness of second-class citizenship. He was truly the Moses of that journey."[10]

In 1958, Howard University named its new law school building in Houston's honor.

William Henry Hastie

William Henry Hastie
(1904–1976)

At Harvard Law School, William Hastie earned top grades, ensuring his election as an editor of the prestigious *Harvard Law Review*. He and the other editors dined together monthly to discuss recent cases and trends in the law. Initially, a white editor from a southern state chose to sit at another table rather than eat with Hastie, an African American. Before long, however, that editor was saving a seat beside him for Hastie.

Throughout a pioneering judicial career, William Hastie commanded respect.

William Henry Hastie was born on November 17, 1904, in Knoxville, Tennessee. His father, William H. Hastie, Sr., studied mathematics at Ohio Wesleyan University and pharmacy at Howard

University. However, as an African American, he could not find a job as either an actuary, someone who deals with insurance matters, or as a pharmacist. He eventually became the first African-American clerk in the U.S. Pension Office.

He married Roberta Childs, a schoolteacher. They bought a chicken farm in the Knoxville suburbs where their son, William, spent his early years. They purchased a horse and buggy so they would not have to ride the segregated streetcar to town.[1]

Roberta Hastie was devoted to her only child. After his birth, she quit teaching. However, she tutored William every day after school. She also told him stories. Fascinated by her stories about the construction of the Panama Canal, William dreamed of becoming an engineer. "I was going to build great canals and dams and stand the whole universe on its head with new and startling things," Hastie later recalled.[2]

William's father stressed strong moral values. In a note to his son he wrote: "Two things . . . should grow stronger in you each day: 1st a desire for well-doing; 2nd a willingness to be guided by your parents."[3]

In 1916 the family moved to Washington, D.C. William attended Garnet Elementary School. The Hasties became close friends of William and Mary Houston, whose son Charles Hamilton Houston was ten years older than young William Hastie. William later acknowledged Charlie Houston's influence. "I followed his footsteps through college and law school, into the practice of law with him and his father, and into law teaching and under his inspiration and leadership, into the struggle to correct the appalling racism of American law."[4]

In 1917, at age twelve, William entered Dunbar High School (formerly M Street High School). The school's all-black faculty taught their students that they could achieve despite racism. The lesson sank in. In 1921, a few months after his father died, William graduated from Dunbar as valedictorian.

William enrolled in Amherst College, Houston's alma mater. At Amherst, African-American students were tolerated in class but were excluded from fraternities, as well as the college's touring orchestras, bands, and glee clubs. During his sophomore year, William wrote a letter of protest to the college president after an article in a student publication used racist language.[5]

William lived and socialized with several other African-American students. He also ran track, placing first, second, or third in most races.

William excelled not only in sports but in academics as well. At Amherst, William won awards for proficiency in Latin, English, mathematics, philosophy, Greek, and physics. He also won the Kellogg Prize and Addison Brown Scholarship, and was elected to Phi Beta Kappa, a national honor society. He was later president of the organization's Amherst chapter.

Hastie graduated from Amherst with highest honors and was the valedictorian of his class. He declined a graduate fellowship abroad and instead taught school to earn money for law school.

In 1927, Hastie entered Harvard Law School. Like Charles Houston, Hastie served as editor of the *Harvard Law Review.* With an A average, he won the respect and admiration of law professors. Professor Felix Frankfurter, who later became a U.S. Supreme Court justice, remembered Hastie as "one of the finest students who has ever studied at Harvard during my time."[6]

In 1930, Hastie graduated near the top of his Harvard Law School class. Back in Washington, D.C., he passed the bar examination. He joined the law firm Houston and Houston and the Howard University Law School faculty. Charles Houston was the law school's vice dean. Howard University was, said Hastie, "the one institution to which a colored man can at present look for an opportunity to teach law."[7] Among Hastie's best students was Thurgood Marshall, who became a leading civil rights lawyer and the first African-American justice on the U.S. States Supreme Court.

On leave from Howard, Hastie worked on his doctorate in law degree. He also worked on an unsuccessful National Association for the Advancement of Colored People (NAACP) lawsuit. It was on behalf of Thomas Hocutt, an African American barred from the University of North Carolina's graduate school. The NAACP later enlisted Hastie to draft antilynching legislation and argue cases involving employment discrimination and equalization of teacher salaries.

In 1933, Hastie became the second African American—Charles Houston was the first—to earn a doctoral degree in juridical science (an advanced degree in the study of law) from Harvard.

That same year, Hastie began a distinguished career in government service. He was named assistant solicitor in the U.S. Department of the Interior. In 1937, President Franklin D. Roosevelt appointed Hastie to the U.S. District Court for the Virgin Islands. He was the first African American to serve on the federal bench.

Hastie briefly returned to Howard Law School as dean before being tapped in 1940 as the first civilian aide to Secretary of War Henry Stimson. To advise Stimson on racial policies in the armed forces, Hastie toured military installations. He found whites-only and blacks-only facilities and fighting units, segregated combat pilot training, whites commanding most black units, and very few African Americans among the ranks of officers and medical and technical personnel. Further, reported Hastie, units led by African Americans were rarely assigned to combat service. He concluded, "[T]he status of the Negro officer is far from what it should be and must be if the Army is to realize the tremendous potential value which the Negro officer represents. . . ."[8]

Hastie opposed Secretary Stimson's stance that African Americans were best suited for menial tasks.

"This attitude," said Hastie, "is the result of wholly unscientific notions that race somehow controls a man's capacity and aptitudes."[9]

In 1943, Hastie resigned from the War Department in protest over plans to establish a separate officers' candidate school for African Americans. He returned to his post as Howard Law School dean.

Later that year, Hastie received the Spingarn Medal, the NAACP's highest honor. The citation noted: "As civilian aide to the Secretary of War, Hastie refused to temporize with racial bigotry, segregation or discrimination."[10]

In 1944 the army integrated officer training. That same year, Hastie joined a campaign for federal legislation against the poll tax, a fee used in southern states to keep poor African Americans from voting.

President Harry Truman appointed Hastie governor of the Virgin Islands in 1946. Two years later Hastie resigned as governor and returned to the United States to aid Truman's reelection effort.

Hastie's work in the campaign was rewarded. During the 1949 congressional recess, President Truman named Hastie to the U.S. Court of Appeals for the Third Circuit. After being sworn in, Hastie became the first African American to serve on the federal appeals court. Senate confirmation was needed to approve the nomination, however. For six months, several senators blocked Hastie's confirmation, falsely alleging that he supported

William Henry Hastie was the first African-American federal judge.
He also served as dean of Howard University Law School.

communism. In 1950 the Senate finally approved
Hastie's lifetime appointment to the federal bench.

Hastie and his family moved to Philadelphia,
Pennsylvania, where the Third Circuit Court of
Appeals convened. In 1943 he had married Beryl
Lockhart and they had two children.

One of the nation's most respected jurists, Hastie
remained a staunch opponent of racial segregation.

He spoke out against housing discrimination and in later years against the black separatist movement. In 1957, he received an honorary doctorate from Yale University, a high compliment for a Harvard alumnus. During the civil rights movement, younger leaders, like the Reverend Martin Luther King, Jr., sought Hastie's advice and support.[11]

In 1968, Hastie became chief judge of the Third Circuit and senior judge in 1971. That same year, he retired from the federal bench.

Hastie received the Philadelphia Award for advancing the community's interest in 1975. He was a member of Omega Psi Phi Fraternity, the National Bar Association, the Washington Bar Association, and the Judicial Conference of the United States.

During his judicial career, Hastie was occasionally mentioned as a possible African-American nominee to the U.S. Supreme Court. In fact, Thurgood Marshall, the eventual nominee, thought that Hastie should have been the first African American appointed to the high court. "He's a great man," said Marshall. "Much better than I ever will be. Honest. His opinions are among the best I've ever read."[12]

William Henry Hastie died on April 14, 1976, in East Norriton, Pennsylvania.

Thurgood Marshall
(1908–1993)

Thurgood Marshall was a mischievous student. At his all-black grade school, teachers sent unruly students to the basement to memorize passages of the Constitution. Often punished, Thurgood read the Constitution aloud again and again until he knew the document by heart.

He applied that knowledge in a brilliant career that spanned more than six decades and culminated with his appointment as a U.S. Supreme Court justice.

Thurgood Marshall was born July 2, 1908, in Baltimore, Maryland. His grandfather and namesake, Thoroughgood Marshall, was a Union soldier in the Civil War. Thurgood's mother, Norma, was a teacher. His father, William, was a waiter on the

Thurgood Marshall

Baltimore & Ohio Railroad and later a steward at an all-white country club.

William Marshall took Thurgood to the railroad station to watch the trains and to the courthouse to hear cases being argued. At home, William taught his two sons to debate and urged them to be proud of their heritage.

When Thurgood was a boy, racism was so harsh that he couldn't even use a rest room in downtown Baltimore. "Trolley cars . . . weren't segregated, [but] everything else was," he later explained.[1]

Thurgood attended all-black Frederick Douglass High School, which was named for the famous antislavery spokesman. In high school Thurgood made good grades, joined clubs, played football, and worked during summers on the Baltimore & Ohio Railroad.

In 1925, with plans to study medicine and dentistry, he entered Lincoln University, a black institution near Philadelphia, Pennsylvania. He and some college friends broke the color barrier at a local movie theater when they dared to sit downstairs in orchestra seats rather than in the balcony designated for African Americans.

On campus Thurgood led the debating team, played fraternity pranks, and after flunking biology changed his major to humanities. For the first time he considered becoming a lawyer. In 1929 he married Vivian Burey, a University of Pennsylvania student. The next year he graduated from Lincoln University.

Barred from attending the all-white University of Maryland Law School, Marshall entered Howard University School of Law in 1930. At Howard he found a mentor in Charles Hamilton Houston, the law school vice dean. Houston taught a course in civil rights law and urged his students to challenge segregation in the courts. The studious Marshall also took courses with William Hastie. Marshall helped Hastie research and write a brief for a case involving an African-American student denied admission to the University of North Carolina Law School. Though Hastie lost the case, Marshall learned a lot about civil rights law.

In 1933, Marshall graduated from law school at the top of his class. He passed the Maryland bar exam and opened a law office in Baltimore. He soon became the attorney for the Baltimore branch of the National Association for the Advancement of Colored People (NAACP).

Marshall's first big civil rights case was a lawsuit filed on behalf of Donald Murray, an African-American student denied admission to the University of Maryland Law School. Marshall asked Charles Houston, then NAACP special counsel, to help him argue against the university's discriminatory policy. Though Marshall and Houston wanted to argue the case in the U.S. Supreme Court, the need did not arise. A Maryland Court of Appeals judge upheld the lower court ruling ordering the law school to admit African Americans.

In 1936, Marshall accepted Houston's invitation to take a so-called temporary assignment as NAACP assistant special counsel. Marshall stayed with the organization twenty-four years.

When Marshall was not working on a trial, he toured the South. He documented discrimination and identified lawyers to try civil rights cases. He looked for teachers, students, and parents who might be willing to sue state and local governments for educational inequities. As a result of this, Marshall sometimes received death threats.

After Houston's departure in 1938, Marshall ran the NAACP legal department. In 1940 he was named director-counsel of the new NAACP Legal Defense and Educational Fund (LDF). The LDF was formed to give legal help to citizens and NAACP branches that had acted against racial injustice.

Marshall, whom African-American newspapers crowned "Mr. Civil Rights," was the nation's leading African-American attorney. Marshall and his team of lawyers successfully challenged segregation on interstate transportation, all-white juries, primary elections, and separate but equal graduate schools.

The LDF defended soldiers in the segregated military, too. They also handled criminal cases, representing civil rights protesters who had been arrested or suspects who had confessed as a result of police beatings. Numerous cases went all the way to the U.S. Supreme Court. Prior to Marshall's Supreme Court appearances, he rehearsed his arguments at Howard with law professors acting as the nine justices. In 1946, Marshall won the Spingarn Medal, the NAACP's highest honor.

By 1950 the NAACP had declared war against racism. Marshall said, "We are going to insist on nonsegregation in American public education from top to bottom—from law school to kindergarten."[2]

Integration was now the goal, and Marshall faced the fight of his life. The battleground was *Brown* v. *Board of Education*, a landmark school desegregation case. In 1950 the NAACP's Topeka, Kansas branch filed a class-action lawsuit. This is a legal action taken by one or more plaintiffs on behalf of themselves and others having the same interest in the alleged wrong. The class-action suit was against Topeka's board of education to integrate the city's elementary schools.

The NAACP enlisted thirteen parents to join the class-action lawsuit on their children's behalf. All the children had been barred from enrolling in the whites-only school nearest their homes. Oliver Brown, the father of Linda Brown, was named lead plaintiff in the case. Though Linda Brown lived just five blocks from a white elementary school, she had to cross railroad tracks and ride a bus twenty-one blocks to a black school.

The U.S. District Court ruled that Topeka's white elementary schools could continue to bar

African Americans. The case reached the U.S. Supreme Court and was combined with similar NAACP school desegregation cases from Delaware, South Carolina, Virginia, and Washington, D.C.

Marshall headed a team of twelve lawyers. He consulted seventy-five leading historians, economists, sociologists, educators, and psychologists. African-American psychologist Kenneth Clark conducted a study of students in segregated South Carolina schools. Using black and white dolls, Clark interviewed sixteen African-American students to determine the effects of segregation.

Responding to questions from Clark, the children said they preferred the white doll. In contrast, they thought the black doll looked "bad." Many students got upset when they admitted that the black doll resembled them. Clark concluded that segregation made African-American children feel inferior.

Armed with Clark's findings and a 235-page brief, the LDF lawyers argued that segregated schools hurt African-American students' self-esteem and deprived students of valuable interaction with one another. Marshall argued that race was not a sound basis for making laws. He also defined equality, explaining, "Equal means getting the same thing, at the same time and in the same place."[3]

After separate hearings in 1952 and 1953, the U.S. Supreme Court issued a unanimous decision in May 1954 in favor of school desegregation. Chief Justice Earl Warren wrote the Court's opinion:

Thurgood Marshall, center, stands with two colleagues following the 1954 Supreme Court decision that found segregation in public schools unconstitutional.

". . . [I]n the field of public education, the doctrine of 'separate but equal' has no place."[4]

The Court's decision found that segregation was unconstitutional because it denied African-American students equal educational opportunities. A year after the Brown ruling, the Court ordered all American school systems to desegregate with deliberate speed.

In February 1955, Marshall's wife, Vivian, died. Later that year, in August, he married Cecilie Suyat, an NAACP secretary. They had two sons.

President John F. Kennedy appointed Marshall to the Second Circuit Court of Appeals in 1962. During Marshall's four years on the federal bench, not one of his majority opinions was overturned by the U.S. Supreme Court. In 1965 he was appointed U.S. solicitor general, the first African American to serve as the nation's top trial attorney.

President Lyndon Johnson named Marshall an associate justice on the U.S. Supreme Court in 1967. He was the first African American to sit on the high court. Associate Justice Marshall defended free speech, the rights of privacy, due process, and civil rights. He staunchly opposed the death penalty.

In 1987, the bicentennial of the Constitution, Marshall declared that the 1787 document was flawed, "requiring several amendments, a civil war and momentous social transformation to attain the system of constitutional government, and its respect for individual freedoms and human rights, we hold as fundamental today."[5]

By 1990, Marshall was one of the few liberals on the Court. A year later, after twenty-four years as an associate justice, Marshall retired from the U.S. Supreme Court. In 1992 he received the Liberty Medal, an international award, for his work to ensure freedom for all Americans. Thurgood Marshall died on January 24, 1993, of heart failure.

Baltimore attorney and NAACP activist Juanita Jackson Mitchell summed up her friend's contribution: "Thurgood was the legal conscience for all Americans. . . ."[6]

4

Constance Baker Motley
(1921–   )

In 1941, Connie Baker was bound for Fisk University in Nashville, Tennessee. On the train ride south, she experienced Jim Crow segregation laws. When the train reached Cincinnati, Ohio, she had to leave her seat and board a rusty, old passenger car reserved for blacks. "I was both frightened and humiliated," she later recalled. "All I knew for sure was that I could do nothing about this new reality."[1] On her return trip north, she brought a Colored Only sign as a souvenir for her parents.

During a pioneering career, Constance Baker Motley challenged racial segregation and broke barriers in the legal profession.

Constance Baker was born September 14, 1921, in New Haven, Connecticut. Her nickname was

Constance Baker Motley

Connie. She was the ninth of twelve children born to Willoughby and Rachel Baker, both immigrants from the island of Nevis in the British West Indies. Willoughby Baker worked as a chef for Skull & Bones, an elite, secret society at Yale University. In addition, he often worked weekends at a hotel or restaurant. Rachel Baker was a homemaker and former seamstress.

The Bakers attended St. Luke's Episcopal Church, where Connie heard Sunday school lectures on African-American history and culture. She found mentors in the pastor, Father John Henry Edwards, and his wife, Merci. They encouraged the youth in the congregation to go to college.[2]

When Connie was growing up, African Americans were only about 2 percent of New Haven's population. The Bakers lived in an integrated neighborhood and Connie, a Girl Scout, attended predominantly white public schools.

Her first experiences with racism occurred outside her community. At age fifteen, Connie and a group of friends picnicking in Bridgeport, Connecticut, were denied admission to a roller-skating rink. Later in Milford, Connecticut, Connie and an interracial group of friends were barred from a public beach.

These incidents awakened Connie to the civil rights struggle. At the same time, she became interested in civic affairs, history, and the legal profession. Articulate and mature for her age, she became president of the New Haven Youth Council and secretary of the New Haven Negro Adult Council. Both organizations addressed civil rights issues.

Connie sold subscriptions for a local black newspaper and read books by African-American scholars, such as W.E.B. Du Bois and James Weldon Johnson. She also read that Abraham Lincoln considered law a difficult profession. Connie believed she could become a lawyer.

At Hillhouse High School, Connie took college preparatory courses, including French and Latin. She competed in basketball and debate. She graduated with honors in 1939. Connie declined a partial scholarship to Dillard University in New Orleans, Louisiana, preferring to attend Fisk University in Nashville, Tennessee.

To save money for college, Connie worked with a National Youth Administration project, refinishing old wooden chairs for fifty dollars a month. In December 1940, however, she met businessman Clarence Blakeslee, a multimillionaire who would change her life.

Blakeslee was concerned that few African Americans used the community center he built, so he arranged a meeting to seek public input. As president of the youth council, Connie attended the meeting and spoke out. Her comments so impressed Blakeslee that he summoned her to his office.

Having reviewed her outstanding high school record, Blakeslee agreed to pay her college tuition.

By February 1941, Connie was enrolled in historically black Fisk University. An economics major, Baker made the honor roll. In 1942 she transferred to New York University and attended classes year-round, graduating in October 1943.

The next year she entered Columbia Law School in New York City. While in law school, she began working as a law clerk for Thurgood Marshall, head of the National Association for the Advancement of Colored People (NAACP) Legal Defense and Educational Fund (LDF). She graduated from law school in June 1946. Blakeslee, whose generosity enabled her to pursue higher education, attended the graduation ceremony.

That same year, Baker married Joel Wilson Motley, a real-estate broker. They had one son.

In 1948, Constance Baker Motley passed the New York State bar examination and began trying LDF cases. She and other LDF lawyers accompanied Marshall when he argued cases before the U.S. Supreme Court.

Motley gained her first courtroom experience in a 1949 case involving equalization of teacher salaries in Jackson, Mississippi. In those days, court appearances by African American and women lawyers were rare. Curiosity seekers came out to see Motley in court.[3]

In 1950, Motley became an LDF assistant counsel. She helped write legal briefs for *Brown* v. *Board of Education,* the landmark school desegregation lawsuit. After the U.S. Supreme Court ruled that "separate but equal" schools were unconstitutional, Motley tackled the difficult legal tasks needed to enforce the decision.

She attacked school segregation at the elementary, high school, and university levels. She represented African-American public school students in Georgia, Florida, Alabama, New York, New Jersey, and Ohio. In 1963 the Birmingham, Alabama, school board expelled 1,100 African-American students for demonstrating in the streets. Through Motley's efforts, the students were quickly reinstated.[4]

Months later, Motley faced off with George Wallace, governor of Alabama, over school desegregation in four counties. Violence erupted in opposition to public school integration, causing some schools to close temporarily. Further, Wallace ordered state troopers to bar African Americans' admission. Finally, the court, backed by a federalized Alabama National Guard, enforced the integration orders.[5]

Motley also helped African-American plaintiffs gain admission to the universities of Alabama, Florida, Georgia, and Mississippi, and Clemson College in South Carolina. In 1961 she sued the University of Georgia for denying admission to

Charlayne Hunter and Hamilton Holmes, both A students from Atlanta. Motley won the case.[6]

In 1961, Motley began work on her most famous case. She represented James Meredith, an African-American student seeking admission to the University of Mississippi. Motley, by then associate counsel for the LDF, worked on the case for nearly a year and a half. Though she won the case, the governor tried to stop Meredith's enrollment. Federal marshals escorted Meredith onto the University of Mississippi campus.

The Meredith case showed Americans "how the system really works," Motley later observed. "Mississippi had long . . . offered the most resistance since the Civil War to the idea of equality for

Constance Baker Motley worked with Thurgood Marshall and other Legal Defense Fund lawyers to put an end to racial segregation.

blacks. . . . [O]ur constitution was put to the test and survived."[7]

Motley also worked in Mississippi with the NAACP field secretary, Medgar Evers (a voting rights advocate slain by a white racist in 1963). In addition, she represented the Reverend Martin Luther King, Jr., after a court order halted his planned march in Albany, Georgia.[8] During her years at the LDF, Motley won nine of the ten cases that she argued before the U.S. Supreme Court.

In 1964, Motley was elected to the New York State Senate. She was the first African-American woman elected senator in the state. In February 1965 the New York City Council elected her to fill a one-year vacancy as Manhattan borough president. She was the first woman and third African American to hold that office.

In November 1965, voters reelected her to a full four-year term. As borough president, she worked to revitalize the inner city, improve city schools, and increase community input in city planning.

President Lyndon Johnson nominated Motley to the Court of Appeals for the Second Circuit in 1966, but withdrew her name under strong opposition to her race and gender. Johnson then appointed Motley to the U.S. District Court for the Southern District of New York, the nation's largest federal trial court. Although some federal judges and southern senators opposed the appointment, the U.S. Senate confirmed Motley. She was the first African-American woman to sit on the federal bench and one of only three women U.S. district judges. In 1982, Motley was named chief judge of her court. Four years later she became senior judge.

Motley owes her success in part to two men—millionaire Clarence Blakeslee, who paid her college tuition, and her mentor, Thurgood Marshall, who hired her at the LDF at a time when woman lawyers had few opportunities. "Thanks to Thurgood Marshall, I was able to get in on the ground floor of the civil rights revolution," she said.[9]

Motley has been inducted into the National Women's Hall of Fame and is listed among *Ebony* magazine's "100 Most Fascinating Black Women of the 20th Century." In 1988 she was awarded the New York State Bar Association Gold Medal. She holds honorary doctorates from many institutions, including Yale University in her hometown.

Decades after fighting some of the key legal battles in the civil rights struggle, Motley still believes that the law is the primary instrument of social reform. "If we have to litigate the basic issues of racial discrimination into the next century," she said, "then that's what we must do."[10]

Benjamin Lawson Hooks

5

Benjamin Lawson Hooks

(1925–   )

During World War II, Benjamin Hooks, then a student at LeMoyne College, was drafted into the U.S. Army. At a military installation in Georgia, he guarded Italian prisoners of war. Ironically, the prisoners were welcome in "whites-only" restaurants that Hooks dared not enter. His duty as a soldier was to defend American freedom and democracy. Yet, African Americans were still treated as second-class citizens in the United States. This blatant injustice left Hooks determined to fight racial bigotry.

Benjamin Lawson Hooks was born January 31, 1925, in Memphis, Tennessee, the fifth of Robert and Bessie Hooks's seven children. The income from Robert Hooks's photography studio provided a comfortable life for his family. During the Depression, however, young Benjamin wore hand-me-down clothes, and Bessie Hooks planned meals that made the grocery money go further. "We were better off than many," Hooks later recalled.[1]

Robert and Bessie Hooks stressed education and community service. A shy youth, Benjamin was expected not only to earn good grades but also to prepare for college.

In segregated Memphis, Tennessee, Benjamin was forced to use "colored-only" bathrooms, lunch counters, water fountains, and other public facilities. He also attended all-black public schools: Porter Elementary School and Booker T. Washington High School. "When I was younger there were not many opportunities for young black people," he said.[2]

Benjamin's boyhood hero was the Reverend G. A. Long, a local minister whose church defied the mayor's order and hosted a speech by African-American labor leader A. Philip Randolph.

Though Robert Hooks shunned organized religion, Benjamin was attracted to the ministry. The elder Hooks advised against that career. After listening to conversations between the African-American professionals—doctors and lawyers—who shared office space with his father, Benjamin decided to become a lawyer.

He graduated from high school in 1941 and entered pre-law studies at LeMoyne College in Memphis. However, he was still shy, especially about speaking in public. Benjamin sometimes wondered if he was suited for the legal profession. In addition, he realized that his parents could not afford to send him to law school.

World War II interrupted Hooks's college education. He was drafted into the U.S. Army. By the time of his discharge at the end of the war, he had achieved the rank of staff sergeant.

Determined to become a lawyer, Hooks left Tennessee, where no law school admitted blacks, and headed to Chicago. Using his GI Bill, a government benefit for military veterans, he was able to pay his law school tuition. In 1946, Hooks entered DePaul University. While in law school, Hooks overcame his shyness, appearing as a guest preacher at a Chicago church.

In 1948 he earned his Juris Doctor degree (equivalent to a bachelor of laws degree). Hooks turned down several well-paying job offers in Chicago and returned to Memphis to join the fight for civil rights. "I knew things could not remain the way they were," he later said, "and that the fight for change would come in the South, so I came back . . . to be a part of that movement."[3]

Back in Memphis, Hooks passed the Tennessee bar examination but found doors in the legal profession closed to African Americans. "When I came back to practice law, there were no opportunities," he said. "I could not get a job as an assistant public defender, assistant county attorney or an assistant prosecutor—the kinds of things that many lawyers do to make a living while they are getting their practices established."[4]

African American lawyers were barred from the law library and white bar associations, and had to use separate rest rooms in the courthouse. Hooks figured he had two choices: "become a worm and succumb or become a man and fight against these things."[5]

Hooks chose to fight. He opened up his own law office but faced prejudice even in the courtroom. "[W]hen I was in court, I was lucky to be called 'Ben.' Usually it was just 'boy,'" he remembered. "[But] the judges were always fair."[6]

In 1949, Hooks met Frances Dancy, a teacher, at the Negro County Fair. They married in 1951 and adopted a daughter.

Hooks became assistant public defender of Shelby County in 1961. As his professional reputation grew, he became more active in religious and civic affairs. He joined the Southern Christian Leadership Conference (SCLC), a civil rights organization cofounded by the Reverend Martin Luther King, Jr. Hooks participated in National Association for the Advancement of Colored People (NAACP) boycotts and restaurant sit-ins.

He was also ordained a Baptist minister. In 1956, Hooks was called to pastor Middle Baptist Church of Memphis, and in 1964 to pastor Detroit's Greater New Mount Moriah Baptist Church as well. He flew to Detroit twice a month to preach.

When Benjamin Hooks encountered racial bias, he concluded that he could either "become a worm and succumb or become a man and fight against these things." His choice was to fight.

Hooks entered politics, too, running unsuccessfully for state legislature in 1954 and for juvenile court judge in 1959 and 1963. Governor Frank G. Clement of Tennessee appointed Hooks to fill a vacancy on the Shelby County criminal court in 1965. Hooks was the first African-American criminal court judge in the state's history.

In 1966, Hooks won election to a full term in office. However, in 1968 he resigned from the judgeship to devote more time to his ministries and to become president of Mahalia Jackson Chicken Systems, Inc., a fast-food chain.

In addition, Hooks made his mark on the local television series: *Conversations in Black and White, The 40 Percent Speak,* and *What Is Your Faith?* Frances Hooks helped her busy husband by serving as his assistant, adviser, secretary, and traveling companion.

In 1968 the Reverend Martin Luther King, Jr., was assassinated. That same year Richard Nixon campaigned for the presidency, promising, among other things, to appoint an African American to the Federal Communications Commission (FCC). The FCC licenses radio and television stations and regulates the broadcasting and telecommunications industries. In 1972, President Nixon named Hooks, who had supported the Republican ticket, to the FCC. Hooks was the first African-American appointee to the seven-member commission.

As an FCC commissioner, Hooks promoted the hiring of minorities in the broadcast industry, encouraged minority ownership of radio and television stations, and advocated more positive images of African Americans in the mass media. During his tenure on the commission, the FCC tried to reduce the barriers in the broadcast industry that had hindered minorities in the past. An office of Equal Employment Opportunity was established, and the number of African Americans employed by the FCC increased from 3 percent to 15 percent.

Hooks resigned from the FCC in 1977 to succeed Roy Wilkins as executive director of the

NAACP, the nation's oldest and largest civil rights group. At the time, the organization was in trouble.

The NAACP's funds were low and its membership had declined from a half million members in the 1950s and 1960s to around two hundred thousand in the late 1970s. Even worse, some people believed that racism was dead and that the NAACP was no longer relevant. Hooks challenged these notions in a speech at the NAACP's 1978 convention in Portland, Oregon.

"Black Americans are not defeated. The civil rights movement is not dead. If anyone thinks that we are going to stop agitating, they had better think again. If anyone thinks that we are going to stop litigating, they had better close the courts. If anyone thinks that we are not going to demonstrate and protest . . . , they had better roll up the sidewalks."[7]

As NAACP executive director, Hooks worked long hours to revitalize the organization. He raised funds, balanced the organization's budget, established communications and religious affairs departments, and reached out to youth and professionals. Under Hooks's leadership, the NAACP more than doubled the number of college chapters and saw membership top five hundred thousand.

Hooks initiated Act-So (Afro-Academic Cultural Technological Scientific Olympics), a nationwide competition for African-American youth. In addition, he focused on voting rights, fair housing, unemployment, and desegregation. Hooks also fought for affirmative action, aid to inner cities, improvements in public education, and an end to apartheid, a racist form of government in South Africa that has since been abolished.

In 1992, Hooks announced plans to resign from the NAACP's top post. Though retired, he continues to pastor. "The church is my first love," he said.[8] He serves on the boards of several institutions, including the National Civil Rights Museum in Memphis. He gives many speeches and has taught at the University of Memphis, home of the Benjamin L. Hooks Institute for Social Change.

Hooks holds honorary doctorate degrees from Howard University, Wilberforce University, and other institutions. In 1986 he was awarded the Spingarn Medal, the NAACP's highest honor.

Hooks said that the civil rights struggle must go on. "[W]e have not yet arrived at equality by any stretch of imagination, and that is what the fight is about today."[9]

6

L. Douglas Wilder
(1931–)

L. Douglas Wilder worked his way through college waiting tables at whites-only country clubs and downtown hotels in Richmond, Virginia. While serving patrons, he sometimes heard them making racist jokes as if he weren't present. He felt outraged.

Later, Wilder broke racial barriers as a politician. In 1989 he was elected governor of Virginia, whose capital city, Richmond, was once known as the capital of the Confederacy.

Lawrence Douglas Wilder was born January 17, 1931. He was the seventh of eight children born to Robert and Beulah Wilder. Robert Wilder sold insurance for the black-owned Southern Aid Insurance Company. His wife was a homemaker.

The Wilder family lived in the city's segregated Church Hill neighborhood. At all-black George

L. Douglas Wilder

Mason Elementary School, Douglas and his fellow students used secondhand textbooks discarded by white schools. He played at colored-only playgrounds, used colored-only rest rooms and drinking fountains downtown, and sat in the back of the streetcar. "When I was coming up," he later recalled, "we didn't even have black policemen."[1]

In the close-knit Church Hill community, Douglas thrived. His father was strict, requiring his children to be mannerly, do chores, and be home on time. Strong and caring, Douglas's mother, Beulah, boosted his self-esteem by telling him he was special. Together they read, worked crossword puzzles, and talked.

Douglas enjoyed teasing his sisters, playing pool and team sports, and joining in friendly arguments. At neighborhood barbershops and shoeshine stands, he honed his debating skills. One barbershop patron joked that Douglas should become a lawyer.

Douglas was raised in what he called "gentle poverty."[2] There was food on the table, music in the house, and flowers in vases, but never any money to spare. To earn money, Douglas shined shoes and worked for the *Richmond Planet*, the city's black newspaper. He sold so many newspapers that he won a weeklong trip to New York. He also ran the elevator at a downtown office building. That job marked his first real encounter with whites.

At Armstrong High School, Douglas earned good grades, acted in plays, was a sergeant in the cadet corps, and played sports. After graduating from high school in 1947, he enrolled in all-black Virginia Union University. Tuition was one hundred dollars a semester. Douglas's mother gave him twenty-five dollars. He had to raise the rest.

During college, he lived at home and waited tables at private clubs and fancy hotels. In 1952 he graduated from Virginia Union University with a bachelor's degree in chemistry.

Douglas worked several odd jobs until the army drafted him in 1952. With the XVII Infantry Regiment's first battalion, he was sent to Inchon, Korea, for combat duty. President Harry Truman's executive order had desegregated the military, but racism persisted within the ranks. Some African Americans in Wilder's battalion charged that discrimination kept them from gaining promotions. Responding to his comrades' outcries, Wilder filed a formal complaint.

In the army Wilder showed not only leadership but also courage. In 1953 while rescuing wounded comrades from Pork Chop Hill, Wilder and a comrade dodged enemy fire and captured nineteen North Korean soldiers by dropping grenades in their bunkers. For his heroism, Wilder was awarded a Bronze Star, one of the U.S. military's highest awards. He was eventually promoted to sergeant.

Back home in Richmond, he applied for a state job as a chemist technician. Because Wilder was African American, the state personnel clerk said the position was filled and offered him a job as cook at a state reform school instead. Wilder turned down the offer. He was later hired as a chemist in the state medical examiner's office.

In 1954 the U.S. Supreme Court ruled in *Brown v. Board of Education* that separate but equal schools were unconstitutional. Inspired by Thurgood Marshall's victory in the landmark school desegregation case, Wilder decided to become a lawyer. "It restored my faith," he later said of the Supreme Court decision.[3]

Denied admission to the University of Virginia, Wilder enrolled in 1956 in Howard University School of Law in Washington, D.C. At Howard, he met undergraduate Eunice Montgomery, whom he married in 1958. They had two daughters and a son before divorcing in 1978.

After law school graduation in 1959, Wilder, his wife, and their firstborn lived with his parents. He passed the Virginia bar exam and opened a law office above a shrimp house in his old Richmond neighborhood. His one-man law firm specialized in personal injury cases, but also tackled tough criminal cases. Wilder represented numerous protesters arrested at civil rights demonstrations. Though not an activist himself, Wilder refused to sit in the "colored" sections of courtrooms and became the first black to join the Richmond Bar Association and a local country club.

Douglas Wilder was the first African American to serve in the Virginia State Senate.

As his caseload increased, his law firm expanded, becoming known as Wilder, Gregory and Associates. "I wanted to be the best lawyer I could be, so that when I walked into the courtroom . . . people would listen and could get results," Wilder later said.[4]

After ten years in the legal profession, he was well respected and wealthy. However, Wilder sometimes accepted more clients than he could adequately represent. As a result, one client sued him, and the Virginia Supreme Court reprimanded him for unprofessional conduct.

In 1969, Wilder entered politics, running for the Virginia State Senate. With the white vote split between two white candidates and the city of Richmond nearly half black, Wilder won the election. He became the first African-American Virginia state senator since Reconstruction.

In the 1970s the maverick senator pushed civil rights legislation. In his first speech on the senate floor, he proposed dropping the state's official anthem, "Carry Me Back to Old Virginny." Its lyrics seemed to glorify slavery. In 1997 the legislature retired the song.

Shrewd and competitive, Wilder fought for fair housing, opposed the death penalty, and waged a nine-year campaign for a Martin Luther King, Jr., holiday. He gradually took more moderate stances and built alliances with other Democrats.

During his five terms, he chaired the Virginia Advisory Legislative Council, the Democratic Steering Committee, and three other major committees: transportation, rehabilitation and social services, and privileges and elections.[5]

After sixteen years in the state senate, Wilder was named one of the five most influential senators. He was ready to make a bid for statewide office. In 1985 he ran for lieutenant governor. He drove three thousand miles around the state, stressing his legislative experience, downplaying civil rights, and saving money for last-minute television advertisements.

The strategy worked. In 1985 he was elected lieutenant governor, becoming the first African-American elected to statewide office in the United States since Reconstruction.

In 1989, Wilder announced his candidacy for governor. He ran unopposed in the Democratic primary and faced Republican J. Marshall Coleman in the general election. Wilder's campaign spotlighted moderate views and his rise from poverty to political prominence.

The campaign spent a record $7 million and targeted white neighborhoods and rural southern Virginia. Although abortion rights was the key campaign issue, race was also an important issue in the election. Wilder, who favored abortion rights, won the historic election by only 6,741 votes. He was the first African American ever elected governor in the United States.

Wilder's inaugural speech in January 1990 offered praise for democracy:

> We mark today not a victory of party or the accomplishments of an individual, but the triumph of an idea—an idea as old as America; as old as the God who looks out for us all. I want [young people] to know: that oppression can be lifted; that discrimination can be eliminated; that poverty need not be binding; that disability can be overcome; And that offer of opportunity in a free society carries with it the requirement of hard work, the rejection of drugs and other false highs,

and a willingness to work with others whatever their color or national origin.[6]

As Virginia's chief executive, Wilder fought crime, increased transportation funding, won congressional approval for a National Air and Space Museum Annex, recruited more minorities and women to public service, and streamlined the Virginia government. Under his leadership, for two consecutive years Virginia was ranked by *Financial World* magazine as the nation's best-managed state.

In 1991 while still governor, Wilder announced his bid for the presidency. Lacking campaign funds, however, he withdrew from the race in January 1992.

Wilder's term as governor expired in 1994. Virginia law bars a governor from serving two terms in a row. Since leaving office, Wilder has practiced law, hosted a radio talk show, taught political science at Virginia Commonwealth University, and launched an effort to establish a museum about slavery in Virginia.[7]

"The fact that I was elected governor should show the people of all communities, especially the Black community, that it can be done," Wilder noted in the year 2000. "I proved that door could be opened."[8]

Barbara Jordan

7

Barbara Jordan
(1936–1996)

Barbara Jordan was accustomed to coming out on top. She had won nearly every speech and debate contest she entered. She expected to be elected freshman class president at Texas Southern University. However, she lost the election to a more popular male candidate. Undeterred, she joined the university's debate and public-speaking teams and became a champion debater.

Barbara Jordan eventually reentered politics, becoming the first African-American woman to serve in the Texas State Senate and the first African-American woman from the South to serve in the U.S. Congress.

Barbara Charline Jordan was born February 21, 1936, in Houston, Texas. She was the youngest of

Benjamin and Arlyne Jordan's three daughters. The family lived in a small house in an all-black neighborhood. Barbara's mother, a homemaker, frequently spoke in church. Her father, a warehouse clerk and part-time Baptist minister, often struggled to make ends meet. The family was poor, but her father ensured they were never hungry, and always had a home to stay in.

Benjamin Jordan wanted his daughters to be prepared for college and he did not allow them to dance, play cards, read fiction or comic books, or go to the movies. He demanded that they study hard, speak clearly, and build their vocabularies. Barbara recited poetry at church programs, sang in the church choir, and played the guitar. She pushed herself to earn A's in school.

Barbara inherited her strong work ethic and her independent streak from her maternal grandfather, John Ed Patten, an avid reader and a junk dealer. He had once been jailed after a wrongful conviction by an all-white jury. His experience gave Barbara a glimpse of racial injustice. She thought segregation was wrong, however, she had little hope that society would change.[1]

On Sunday afternoons Barbara helped her grandfather sort through the junk to sell from his mule-drawn wagon. She received not only a share of the profits but also priceless wisdom. Her grandfather taught Barbara to think for herself and strive to be outstanding.

Barbara was president of the honor society at Houston's all-black Phyllis Wheatley High School. She considered being a pharmacist but changed her mind after an African-American woman lawyer spoke at the school's career day. Barbara, then a sophomore, decided to pursue law, a profession dominated by white men.

On the high school speech team, she developed the public-speaking skills that she would later use in court and politics. During her senior year, she was named Girl of the Year by Zeta Phi Beta sorority, a national black sorority. Barbara also won the nationwide Ushers Oratorical Contest for African-American students. To compete in Chicago, she took her first train ride.

In a post-victory interview with the *Houston Informer*, Barbara put her accomplishment in perspective. "It's just another milestone I have passed; it's just the beginning."[2]

In 1952, Barbara graduated from high school at sixteen and entered all-black Texas Southern University. She lived at home so her parents could save money for law school. She became the first woman on the university's debate team. The team competed not only against all-black schools but against other major universities as well. Barbara was eventually elected team president.

While traveling to debates, she noticed that segregation, though widespread, was not as severe in the North as in the South. In 1954 the U.S. Supreme

Court ruled in *Brown* v. *Board of Education* that separate but equal schools were unconstitutional. Barbara began to believe that racial integration was possible.

In 1956, Jordan graduated with honors from Texas Southern with a double major in history and political science. She entered Boston University Law School. She was one of only two African-American women in the first-year class of about six hundred. She studied hard to keep up in class. "The most important lesson was that you always had to be prepared," Jordan later wrote.[3] In 1959 she earned her law degree and passed the Massachusetts bar examination.

Jordan declined a job offer from an insurance company and returned to Texas to set up her own law practice—in her parents' dining room. With few clients, she supplemented her income by working as an administrative assistant for a judge. In her spare time she volunteered in John F. Kennedy's presidential campaign. Jordan stuffed envelopes, licked stamps, made phone calls, and organized meetings. One night she filled in for another speaker. Her words so moved the audience that from then on, she gave the speeches for the Harris County Democratic party.

The civil rights movement was in full swing. The pace of change, however, was too slow for Jordan. She was convinced that the only way to speed up progress was to become a lawmaker.

In 1962 and 1964 she ran unsuccessfully for the Texas House of Representatives but won a seat in 1966 in the all-white, all-male Texas Senate. She represented a newly drawn district including blacks, migrant workers, and pro-labor whites.

The first African American to serve in the Texas Senate since the 1880s, Jordan was also the first African-American woman ever elected to the Texas Senate. Her fellow senators nominated her Outstanding Freshman Senator. Her colleagues later elected her president pro tem of the state senate, enabling her to serve as governor for a day.

In Jordan's two terms as state senator, half the bills she sponsored—including the state's first minimum wage law and legislation establishing the Texas Fair Employment Practices Commission—were passed into law.

While Jordan was a state senator, President Lyndon Johnson, a fellow Texan and civil rights advocate, became her political mentor. At her 1971 campaign fund-raiser, he noted, "Barbara Jordan proved to us that black is beautiful before we knew what it meant."[4]

In 1972, Jordan was elected to represent the Eighteenth District of Texas in the U.S. House of Representatives. She was the first African-American woman to represent a southern state in Congress. She served on several important congressional committees, including the House Committee on Government Operations and the House Judiciary

Barbara Jordan fought to extend voting rights legislation to make voting more accessible to minorities.

Committee. Jordan sponsored legislation extending voting rights' protection to poor citizens and those who did not speak English. She also authored the Jordan Amendment, requiring schools or companies that receive government funds to use the money in a nondiscriminatory manner.

Jordan was a true patriot. She got goose bumps when she heard the national anthem and always carried a copy of the Constitution. Love of country guided her during the Judiciary Committee's 1974 Watergate hearings. The committee had to decide whether to recommend the impeachment of President Richard Nixon for his reelection campaign committee's break-in at Democratic party offices. During an impeachment, the U.S. House of Representatives presents formal charges against a public official. If the House votes to impeach, a trial by the U.S. Senate decides whether to remove the public official from office.

In a speech during the Watergate hearings, Jordan declared, "My faith in the Constitution is whole, it is complete, it is total and I am not going to sit here and be an idle spectator to the diminution, the subversion, the destruction of the Constitution."[5]

Jordan concluded that Congress should move to impeach. Her stunning speech landed her in the national spotlight as a rising political star.

Two years later Jordan addressed the 1976 Democratic National Convention, the first African-American to keynote a national party convention. Rumors swirled that Jordan might be tapped as vice-presidential running mate, a cabinet member, or ambassador. Instead, she was reelected to Congress.

In 1977 she gave the commencement address at Harvard University, which two decades earlier had rejected her law school application. "What the people want is simple," she explained. "They want an America as good as its promise."[6]

In 1978, Jordan retired from Congress and returned to Texas. She taught at the Lyndon B. Johnson School of Public Affairs at the University of Texas in Austin.

She also continued to advise leading politicians. She keynoted the 1992 Democratic National Convention and chaired the 1995 Commission for Immigration Reform.

During her career, she received many honors: almost thirty honorary doctorate degrees, induction into the National Women's Hall of Fame, and nomination by *World Almanac* as one of the twenty-five most influential American women. In 1994, President Bill Clinton awarded her the Presidential Medal of Freedom, the country's highest civilian honor.

In later years Jordan suffered from multiple sclerosis and eventually needed a wheelchair. Barbara Jordan died on January 17, 1996, of viral pneumonia, a complication of leukemia. She was buried at the Texas National Cemetery, the first African American to be so honored.

8

Johnnie Cochran
(1937–   )

Even as a boy, Johnnie Cochran sensed there was a big world beyond his backyard. He thumbed through the *Encyclopedia Britannica* and dreamed of visiting far-off places.[1] With his family, he window-shopped at Crenshaw Shopping Center, America's first shopping mall.

At the homes of wealthy teenage friends, he saw marble staircases, swimming pools, tennis courts, and archery ranges. Johnnie desired such luxuries and believed that he could have them one day, if he set goals and worked hard.[2] He went on to become one of the most famous and successful lawyers in the United States.

Johnnie Cochran was born October 2, 1937, in Shreveport, Louisiana. His father, Johnnie Cochran,

Johnnie Cochran

Sr., moved the family to San Francisco, California, in search of better economic opportunities. Johnnie, the older brother to two sisters, was just five years old. His mother, Hattie, sold Avon cosmetics part-time. His father worked at a shipyard. Later he worked as a salesman and manager for Golden State Mutual Insurance Company, then one of the nation's largest black-owned businesses.

In the integrated schools Johnnie excelled, skipping second grade and earning mostly A's. His childhood heroes included heavyweight boxing champion Joe Louis and baseball great Jackie Robinson, athletes who symbolized African-American achievement.[3]

In 1948 the family moved to the San Diego area and in 1949 to Los Angeles. The family bought a house in the West Adams neighborhood, and Johnnie attended integrated schools. However, he experienced racial discrimination on summer trips back to Louisiana. There, he used the "colored-only" facilities. He didn't really understand racial segregation, but he never forgot it.

Johnnie's parents wanted him to become a doctor. In junior high school, however, he decided he wanted to become a lawyer. At exclusive Los Angeles High School, Johnnie joined the debate team, played football, studied Spanish, French, and Italian, and was inducted into the Honor Society. As a teen, he worked for a dry cleaner, a caterer, and as a paperboy.

Attorney Thurgood Marshall's victory in the landmark 1954 school desegregation case *Brown* v. *Board of Education* sealed Johnnie's ambitions. The dream of becoming a lawyer, said Cochran, "found its wings in Thurgood Marshall's epic victory for justice."[4]

Cochran graduated from Los Angeles High in 1955 and entered the University of California Los Angeles (UCLA), where he joined the Kappa Alpha Psi fraternity and majored in business administration. While in college, he worked for his father, selling insurance, and as a mail sorter for the U.S. Postal Service.

In 1959, Cochran entered Loyola Marymount Law School. The following summer he married Barbara Berry. They had two daughters before divorcing in 1977. Cochran later had a son, and married Sylvia Dale.

During his third year of law school, Cochran was hired as the first African-American clerk in the Los Angeles city attorney's office. He graduated from law school in 1962. After passing the California bar examination in 1963, he became a deputy city attorney.

Cochran prosecuted criminal cases, sometimes African-American male defendants beaten by police during the course of arrest. Cochran felt torn between his professional responsibilities and his commitment to civil rights. "My conscience gave me no peace," he said.[5] Eventually, Cochran requested that he not be assigned to prosecute these cases.

In 1965 he left the city attorney's office and entered private practice with Gerald Lenoir, also a former deputy district attorney. Cochran was determined to work within the legal system to effect change. In 1966 he struck out on his own, renting office space on Los Angeles's prestigious Wilshire Boulevard.

Cochran's first big case was representing the widow of Leonard Deadwyler. He was an African-American motorist shot dead in May 1966 by a Los Angeles police officer during a traffic stop. At the time, Deadwyler was speeding his pregnant wife to the hospital. The officer who fired the fatal shots said he acted in self-defense. Cochran lost the wrongful death case, but he garnered considerable publicity. By the end of 1966, Nelson L. Atkins and Irwin Evans had joined Cochran as law partners.

Cochran grabbed headlines again in 1970 when he represented Elmer "Geronimo" Pratt, a Vietnam veteran accused of murdering a young schoolteacher. Pratt was a former member of the Black Panther party, a militant, grassroots organization that advocated self-help and self-defense. Although the victim's husband identified another person as the assailant, Pratt was convicted and given a life sentence. Convinced that justice had been denied, Cochran vowed to press for a retrial and work for Pratt's release.

In 1977, Cochran was named Criminal Trial Lawyer of the Year. The following year he became assistant district attorney for Los Angeles County, the first African American in that post. In 1979 the California Trial Lawyers Association named him the outstanding law enforcement officer.

That same year, he was driving his Rolls-Royce when Los Angeles police officers pulled him over for a traffic stop. They ordered Cochran and his daughters out of the car, drew guns, and searched the car. The police found his district attorney's badge, apologized, and drove away. "Race plays a part in almost every aspect of America," Cochran said.[6]

In 1981 he returned to private practice and won numerous landmark decisions in police misconduct cases. He represented the family of Ron Settles, an African-American college football star arrested for speeding and found dead in his jail cell. Police tried to make his death look like a suicide. However, Cochran ordered a second autopsy that showed Settles was strangled by a police choke hold. The Settles family was awarded a $760,000 settlement, and the Los Angeles Police Department outlawed the choke hold.

In 1992, Cochran won $9.4 million, the highest jury award in Los Angeles history, in the case of a thirteen-year-old Latina girl molested by a police officer.

By 1995, Cochran had won more than $40 million in judgments against California municipalities

Johnnie Cochran is best known for defending O.J. Simpson. Before Simpson's case, Cochran had made a name for himself defending the underdog.

and police departments. Cochran's annual salary was estimated at nearly $1 million.

Cochran's fame grew as he represented celebrity clients, such as pro football player Jim Brown, pop singer Michael Jackson, and rapper and music producer Sean "Puffy" Combs.

Well connected among Los Angeles leaders, Cochran is the only attorney ever to receive the Trial Lawyer of the Year Award from both the Los Angeles Trial Lawyers Association and the Criminal Courts Bar Association. He has been inducted into the Inner Circle of Advocates, an organization of the country's top one hundred plaintiff attorneys, and the American College of Trial Lawyers, which includes the top one percent of trial attorneys in the United States.

Charming and persuasive, Cochran is cool, confident, captivating, and calculating in the courtroom. He does his homework and has amazing recall of facts and case law. With flawless preparation and a flair for drama, he delivers impassioned legal arguments in a style reminiscent of Baptist preachers and stage actors.

Television audiences met Cochran in 1995 during what became known as "The Trial of the Century"—the murder trial of former pro football player and sports commentator O. J. Simpson. Simpson pleaded innocent to charges of fatally stabbing his ex-wife Nicole Brown Simpson and her friend Ron Goldman. Cochran led the so-called Dream Team of high-priced lawyers who defended Simpson.

Cochran's legal team questioned the prosecution's timeline of the murder, charged law enforcement officers with sloppy police work, and raised suspicions about evidence planting. Cochran's team also exposed the racist sentiments of Mark Fuhrman, an officer assigned to the case.

During the trial, district attorney Christopher Darden asked Simpson to try on the leather glove worn during the murder. The glove, stiffened by dried blood, did not appear to fit Simpson's hand. Citing faulty evidence such as the glove, Cochran's closing argument claimed that a racist police officer had framed Simpson. Cochran urged the jury, "If it doesn't fit, you must acquit."[7]

The jury found Simpson not guilty, a controversial and divisive verdict that was widely applauded by many blacks and assailed by many whites.

After the Simpson trial, Cochran hosted the Court TV show *Cochran and Company*, later renamed *Johnnie Cochran Tonight*. He lived part-time in New York, where the show was produced. He joined the legal teams representing police brutality victim Abner Louima, who was beaten and sexually assaulted by police, and the family of Amadou Diallo, an unarmed man fatally shot by New York police.

In 1997, Cochran finally resolved the seemingly hopeless case of former Black Panther Geronimo Pratt, who had spent twenty-seven years in prison. Finding that a chief prosecution witness, an FBI informant, lied under oath, the California Superior Court overturned the murder conviction and freed Pratt.

In 1999, Cochran's Los Angeles law firm joined a leading New York personal injury firm in forming the Cochran Firm/Schneider, Kleinick, Weitz, Damashek & Shoot. Cochran quit his television show to work on the new venture. In 2001 he joined the Reparations Assessment Group to devise legal strategies to gain reparations for slavery.

"All I've ever wanted to do is help the oppressed and disenfranchised," Cochran said.[8]

Marian Wright Edelman

9

Marian Wright Edelman
(1939–   )

During the 1940s and 1950s, life was hard for African Americans in segregated Bennettsville, South Carolina. They could not use public parks, playgrounds, or swimming pools. Nor could they eat at lunch counters. Segregation sent a message that blacks were inferior to whites and, thus, less worthy of rights and privileges.

Marian Wright Edelman's parents told her that she was just as good as anybody else. They also stressed that no task was below her and that community service was her Christian duty. "That taught me, if you don't like the way the world is, you change it," Marian later recalled.[1] She took these lessons to heart.

Founder and president of the Children's Defense Fund, Marian Wright Edelman is one of America's leading advocates for children and families.

Born June 6, 1939, in Bennettsville, South Carolina, Marian was the youngest of Arthur and Maggie Wright's five children. Arthur Wright pastored Shiloh Baptist Church, and Maggie Wright played the church organ and raised funds. Because segregation laws barred blacks from public parks, the Reverend Wright built a playground, skating rink, and canteen for African Americans behind his church. He established, and his wife ran, the Wright Home for the Aged. The couple also cared for twelve foster children.

Marian and her sister and brothers followed their parents' example of helping the less fortunate. "We learned that service is the rent you pay for living," Marian later wrote.[2]

Her childhood, however, was not all work. Nicknamed Booster, Marian took piano and voice lessons, was a Brownie Girl Scout, and enjoyed reading and going to movies. She also saw speeches and performances by African-American role models, such as her namesake, opera singer Marian Anderson. Marian's bubbly personality won friends.

Her happy childhood was marred by racism, however. One incident haunted her years later.[3] An African-American migrant family's car collided with a truck on the highway that passed the Wrights' home. The black accident victims appeared seriously injured. When a whites-only ambulance arrived, its white driver, finding the white truck driver unharmed, drove off, leaving the migrant family bleeding in the road.

In 1954, Marian and her father awaited the U.S. Supreme Court ruling in *Brown* v. *Board of Education*, the landmark school desegregation case. The Reverend Wright suffered a fatal heart attack days before the historic decision was handed down. As he lay dying, he urged fourteen-year-old Marian, "Don't let anything get in the way of your education."[4]

From first through twelfth grade, Marian attended Marlboro Training School, the local school for black children. There, she earned good grades and was a drum majorette with the band. Marian graduated from high school in 1956, hoping to follow her sister, Olive, to Fisk University in Tennessee. However, Spelman College, an all-black woman's college in Atlanta, Georgia, offered her a full scholarship.

Though the socially conservative woman's college was not Marian's first choice, she came to love Spelman. She heard prominent African Americans such as Martin Luther King, Jr., speak at chapel. At the end of her sophomore year, she won a scholarship to study in France, Switzerland, and Russia. The experience boosted her self-confidence and broadened her horizons. She decided to pursue a foreign service career.

Those plans changed, however, when Marian returned to Spelman and joined the civil rights movement. Along with thirteen other Spelman students, she was arrested at a sit-in at the City Hall cafeteria. Afterward, she volunteered at the Atlanta office of the National Association for the Advancement of Colored People (NAACP). Sensing a need, Marian decided to become a lawyer to help fight for racial equality. In 1960 she graduated from Spelman as valedictorian and won a John Hay Whitney Fellowship to attend Yale University Law School.

While at Yale, Wright went to Mississippi to help the Student Nonviolent Coordinating Committee (SNCC) register African-American voters. She graduated from law school in 1963 and landed an internship with the NAACP Legal Defense and Educational Fund. After a year of training at the fund's New York City office, Wright set up a law office in Jackson, Mississippi, to handle civil rights cases. Many civil rights protesters were arrested. "That summer I very seldom got a client out of jail who had not been beaten by white police officers," she recalled.[5]

Upon passing the Mississippi bar exam in 1965, Wright became the first African-American woman lawyer in the state. In addition, she became director of Mississippi's NAACP Legal Defense and Educational Fund.

In 1965, Wright helped the Child Development Group of Mississippi obtain a federal Head Start grant to serve preschool children of poor families. She convinced four senators, including Robert

Kennedy of New York, to visit Mississippi to see the poverty and hunger firsthand. Through these efforts, she met Peter Edelman, a Jewish Harvard-trained lawyer who was Kennedy's legislative aide.

In 1968, Wright moved to Washington, D.C., and established the Washington Research Project to work for social justice. She helped coordinate the Poor People's Campaign, a mass demonstration planned by the Reverend Martin Luther King, Jr., before his April 1968 assassination.

In July 1968, Wright married Peter Edelman. Theirs was one of the first interracial marriages in Virginia after the U.S. Supreme Court struck down the law forbidding interracial unions. The couple has three sons.

In 1969 the Washington Research Project pushed for more federal funding for the education of poor children. In 1971 the Edelmans moved to Boston, where Marian headed the Harvard Center for Law and Education. She flew back and forth to the nation's capital to oversee the Washington Research Project. In 1979 the Edelmans moved back to Washington, D.C.

In 1973, Marian Wright Edelman founded the Children's Defense Fund (CDF), a Washington-based child advocacy group that highlights children's needs, lobbies lawmakers and policymakers, and encourages community self-help initiatives. With the motto, "Leave no child behind,"[6] the CDF addresses children's needs in the areas of health care, education, crime prevention, teen pregnancy prevention, and family welfare. "Investing in children is not a national luxury or a national choice," Edelman insisted. "It's a national necessity."[7]

The CDF's research revealed that one in five American children is poor, one in six has no health insurance, and one in eight never graduates from high school.[8] Every minute a baby is born to a teen mother, and every two hours a child or youth under twenty is killed by a firearm.[9]

These grim statistics fuel Edelman's commitment to children's causes. In legislative battles, she has won both liberal and conservative support and has gained

Marian Wright Edelman founded the Children's Defense Fund. The fund represents the interests of children and lobbies legislators to pass laws for their benefit.

a reputation as one of the most influential and effective lobbyists on Capitol Hill. She and her staff help draft legislation, testify in congressional hearings, and monitor federal agencies' compliance with the law.

In 1983 she launched her most ambitious effort to date—a nationwide teen pregnancy prevention campaign to reduce the number of children born in poverty.

Edelman, a tireless crusader for children, made passage of a comprehensive child care bill a legislative priority in 1988. Two years later, Congress finally passed a $600 million child care bill. In 1992 the Bush administration approved a $200 million increase in the federal Head Start program. "Our problem is not one of law," Edelman noted, "but of making laws work, getting them funded, riding the bureaucrats and enabling people to take advantage of what Congress intended."[10]

With a $10 million budget and more than one hundred employees, the CDF itself has never accepted government grants and is funded entirely by private foundations and individuals. In the 1990s the CDF broadened its scope to address child care, child health, child welfare and mental health, violence prevention, youth development, and family income. In June 1996 the Children's Defense Fund spearheaded a national movement, called Stand for Children, that brought three hundred thousand supporters to a Washington, D.C., rally.

Edelman's visionary leadership has also benefited her alma mater, Spelman College. She served as a trustee from 1976 to 1987, and in 1980 became the first African-American woman to chair the board. Edelman was also the first African-American woman elected to the Yale University Corporation.

In 1992, Edelman added best-selling author to her list of accomplishments. Her books include *A Measure of Our Success: A Letter to My Children and Yours; Guide My Feet: Meditations and Prayers on Loving and Working for Children;* and *Lanterns: A Memoir of Mentors.*

Edelman holds numerous honorary doctorate degrees and has received many honors, including a MacArthur Foundation Prize Fellowship, the Albert Schweitzer Humanitarian Prize, the Ghandi Peace Prize, and the Robert F. Kennedy Lifetime Achievement Award.

In 2000, Edelman received the Presidential Medal of Freedom, the nation's highest civilian award. "Like her namesake, Marian's voice is always strong and true, singing that we are all children of God and, therefore, must protect all our children," President Bill Clinton stated, comparing Edelman to opera singer Marian Anderson.[11]

10

Carol Moseley-Braun
(1947–)

Carol Moseley-Braun never hesitated to stand up for justice, though she knew that working for unpopular causes could be dangerous. In her elementary classroom, she hid under a desk while protesters threw rocks at the newly integrated school. In her teens, she once again faced rock throwers when she spread her towel on a newly desegregated Chicago beach.

These experiences inspired the trailblazing political career that carried Moseley-Braun to Capitol Hill as the first African-American woman in the U.S. Senate.

Carol Moseley was born August 16, 1947, in Chicago, Illinois, the first of Joseph and Edna Davie Moseley's four children. Her father was a policeman

Carol Moseley-Braun

and later a real estate agent. Her mother was a medical technician. The family owned and lived in an apartment building in a middle-class neighborhood on Chicago's South Side.

At the family's home, Joseph Moseley, a frustrated jazz musician, welcomed musician friends of different racial and ethnic backgrounds. From her father, Carol learned that prejudice was wrong.

Carol's mother encouraged her to work hard, do her best, and believe in herself. Edna Moseley told her daughter she could do anything.

Carol's father was active in organized labor and civic affairs. Accompanying him to political meetings, Carol saw democracy at work.

Her father was troubled, however. He sometimes had violent outbursts and beat his children with a rope. In 1963 when Carol was fifteen, her parents divorced. Edna Moseley and the children moved in with their grandmother in a violent, slum neighborhood known as Bucket of Blood. The family stayed there for two years.

To help her family escape the poverty and hopelessness, Carol worked part-time at a grocery store during high school. "I had to grow up fast," she later said.[1]

While at Parker High School, Carol became emboldened by the civil rights movement that was sweeping the country. At a lunch counter where she was refused service, she staged a one-person sit-in. When she was finally served, she paid for the cup of coffee and left without drinking it. And, at sixteen, she marched with Martin Luther King, Jr., in an all-white Chicago neighborhood to press for housing integration.

Carol majored in political science at the University of Illinois, Chicago. To help pay for college, she worked in the post office. She also worked for state representative Harold Washington, who eventually became Chicago's first African-American mayor.

She graduated in 1969 with a bachelor's degree. She then entered the University of Chicago Law School, where she organized a chapter of the Black Law Students Association. She earned her Juris Doctor degree (equivalent to a bachelor of laws degree) in 1972.

The following year Carol Moseley married attorney and former law school classmate Michael Braun. They have one son, Matthew, born in 1976. The couple divorced in 1986.

From 1973 to 1977, Moseley-Braun worked as an assistant U.S. attorney in the U.S. District Court of Illinois. While there, she received the U.S. Attorney General's Special Achievement Award. After her son's birth, she worked briefly at a Chicago law firm.

In 1978, Moseley-Braun left a promising legal career to run for state representative. She won her first political contest and was reelected four times, serving ten years in the Illinois House of

Representatives. "It was immediately obvious that Carol was in her element," said former legislative aide Sue Purrington. "She liked the power play and the control."[2]

As a legislator, Moseley-Braun was known as much for boldness, independence, and integrity as she was for her warm personality and beaming smile. She advocated tirelessly for women, minorities, and the poor. "I've always felt my obligation—my calling—is to use my talents on behalf of the public interest," said Moseley-Braun.[3]

A tough debater, she supported fair housing, gun control, and reform in education, welfare, and health care. She fought the death penalty. A Democrat herself, she filed and won a 1980 lawsuit against the Democratic party over a redistricting plan that threatened to decrease African-American and Latino representation on Chicago's South Side. Annually, the citizens' group Independent Voters of Illinois cited her among the best legislators.

As her reputation grew, so did her influence, fueled by her ability to build coalitions. In 1980, Moseley-Braun made history in Illinois, becoming the state's first African American and first woman to serve as assistant house majority leader. In 1983, Chicago Mayor Harold Washington named Moseley-Braun his floor leader in the legislature, despite her lack of seniority among the Chicago delegation.

She sometimes differed with Mayor Washington's legislative agenda. These differences ultimately provoked Washington to block Moseley-Braun's anticipated 1986 run for lieutenant governor.

That same year, she and Michael Braun divorced, her mother suffered a severe stroke, and her father and brother died. Moseley-Braun turned to her religious faith for strength and renewal. "My faith is as much a part of me as my name," she later stated.[4]

In 1987, with Mayor Harold Washington's blessing, Moseley-Braun successfully ran for Cook County recorder of deeds. The first African American ever elected to an executive post in the county, she oversaw three hundred employees and an $8 million budget. By the end of her four-year term, Moseley-Braun had computerized and restructured the agency and nearly ended corruption and political patronage by enforcing a code of ethics.

Despite her accomplishments as recorder of deeds, Moseley-Braun chose not to seek reelection. Like millions of Americans, she watched the Senate confirmation hearings for U.S. Supreme Court nominee Clarence Thomas, a conservative African-American federal judge.

During the televised hearings, Thomas's former colleague Anita Hill, a law professor, accused him of sexual harassment. Despite Hill's charges and protests from civil rights and women's groups, the all-white, all-male Senate Judiciary Committee sent the nomination to the full Senate for a vote. Thomas was confirmed as a Supreme Court justice.

Moseley-Braun was outraged that two-term Senator Alan Dixon, a Democrat from Illinois, voted to confirm Thomas. Throughout the country, the public mood turned against incumbent senators. Illinois voters launched a "Draft Moseley-Braun" movement. She decided to challenge Dixon in the U.S. Senate race in 1992.

As the incumbent, Dixon had the Democratic party's backing. Moseley-Braun waged a low-budget, grassroots primary campaign that defeated both incumbent Dixon and multimillionaire Al Hofeld. As Moseley-Braun spread her message of change, her support grew. "It's a historic candidacy and we're looking to make history," she declared.[5]

Scandals, however, threatened to erode the comfortable lead she enjoyed. Braun was linked romantically to her campaign manager, Kgosie Matthews. She was accused of mishandling funds that her mother owed Medicaid for nursing home care. Moseley-Braun admitted her mistake and repaid Medicaid. Moseley-Braun won the November 1992 general election with 53 percent of the vote. She became the first African-American woman to serve in the U.S. Senate.

The only African American in the Senate, Moseley-Braun was appointed to the Judiciary Committee. In 1993 she single-handedly opposed an amendment to extend a design patent for the emblem of the United Daughters of the Confederacy. The emblem featured the flag of

Carol Moseley-Braun was the first African-American U.S. Senator.

the Confederate States of America, a symbol some Americans view as racist. This troubled Moseley-Braun. After the Senate voted 52–48 to extend the patent, she rose to her feet with a fiery appeal.

". . . [I]n spite of the fact that we have made strides forward, . . . there are those of us who would keep slipping back into the darkness of division, into the snake pit of racial hatred, of racial antagonism and of support for symbols—symbols of the struggle to keep African-Americans . . . in bondage."[6]

Moseley-Braun's passionate speech moved her Senate colleagues to vote again and reject the patent extension 75–25.

In the Senate, Moseley-Braun was the first and only woman to serve as a permanent member of the powerful Senate Finance Committee. She also served on the Banking, Housing, and Urban Affairs Committee, the Small Business and Aging committees, and the bipartisan commission on Entitlements and Tax Reform.

Her legislative initiatives included school and library renovation, women's pension equity, and historic preservation of the Underground Railroad. "I was able to speak up for women when the issue was retirement security," said Moseley-Braun, "and could advocate the interest of African Americans when the issues were about social and economic integration."[7]

During her term, she drew criticism for meeting privately with a Nigerian military dictator. Like her initial Senate bid, her 1998 reelection campaign was marred by scandals ranging from a trip to Africa to campaign fund-raising. Moseley-Braun lost her Senate seat.

She was serving as a consultant to the U.S. Department of Education in 1999 when President Bill Clinton nominated her as ambassador to New Zealand and Samoa. The Senate voted 98–2 to confirm her nomination. "The Senate's overwhelming bipartisan vote is a strong endorsement of her outstanding experience and credentials for the position," Clinton stated.[8] In 1999, Moseley-Braun was sworn in as ambassador.

Chapter Notes

Chapter 1. Charles Hamilton Houston

1. Genna Rae McNeill, *Groundwork: Charles Hamilton Houston and the Struggle for Civil Rights* (Philadelphia: University of Pennsylvania Press, 1983), p. 42.

2. Ibid., p. 64.

3. Columbus Salley, *The Black 100* (Seacaucus, N.J: Citadel Press, 1993), p. 25.

4. Barbara Carlisle Bigelow, ed., *Contemporary Black Biography, Vol. 4* (Detroit: Gale Research, 1993), p. 126.

5. Peter B. Levy, *Let Freedom Ring: A Documentary History of the Modern Civil Rights Movement* (New York: Praeger Publishers, 1992), p. 30.

6. McNeill, p. 139.

7. Ibid., pp. 144–145.

8. Ibid., pp. 152, 154.

9. "Charles Hamilton Houston," "Charles Hamilton Houston Bar Association," n.d. <http://www.charleshouston.org/chhbio.html> (March 17, 2001).

10. Geraldine R. Segal, *Blacks in the Law: Philadelphia and the Nation* (Philadelphia: University of Pennsylvania Press, 1983), p. 211.

Chapter 2. William Henry Hastie

1. Gilbert Ware, *William Hastie: Grace Under Pressure* (New York: Oxford University Press, 1984), p. 4.

2. Ibid., p. 34.

3. Ibid., p. 5.

4. Geraldine Segal, *In Any Fight Some Fall* (Rockville, Md.: Mercury Press, 1975), p. 5.

5. Ware, pp. 12–14.

6. Walter White, *A Man Called White* (New York: Viking Press, 1948), p. 156.

7. Ware, p. 48.

8. Anna Rothe, ed., *Current Biography 1944* (New York: H. W. Wilson Company, 1944), p. 278.

9. Ibid.

10. Ibid., p. 279.

11. Erica Chadbourne, *The High Mountain: William Henry Hastie* (Cambridge, Mass.: Harvard College, 1984), Exhibition Catalog Items #166 and 167, unpaginated.

12. Howard Ball, *A Defiant Life: Thurgood Marshall and the Persistence of Racism in America* (New York: Crown Publishers, 1998), p. 46.

Chapter 3. Thurgood Marshall

1. Juan Williams, "The Thurgood Marshall Nobody Knows," *Ebony*, May 1990, p. 69. Reprinted from the *Washington Post*.

2. James Haskins, *Thurgood Marshall: A Life for Justice* (New York: Henry Holt, 1992), p. 84.

3. Ibid., p. 93.

4. Supreme Court of the United States, *Brown* v. *Board of Education of Topeka*, 347 U.S. 483 (1954).

5. Haskins, pp. 141, 143.

6. Michael D. Davis and Hunter R. Clark, *Thurgood Marshall: Warrior at the Bar, Rebel on the Bench* (New York: Birch Lane Press, 1992), p. 372.

Chapter 4. Constance Baker Motley

1. Constance Baker Motley, *Equal Justice Under Law: An Autobiography* (New York: Farrar, Straus and Giroux, 1998), pp. 47–48.

2. Jessie Carney Smith, ed., *Notable Black American Women, Vol. 2* (Detroit: Gale Research, 1992), p. 779.

3. Marie Brenner, "Judge Motley's Verdict," *The New Yorker*, May 16, 1994, p. 68.

4. Charles Moritz, ed., *Current Biography 1944* (New York: H. W. Wilson Company, 1944), pp. 306–307.

5. Ibid., p. 307.

6. Motley, pp. 145-146.

7. Henry Hampton and Steve Fayer with Sarah Flynn, *Voices of Freedom: An Oral History of the Civil Rights Movement from the 1950s Through the 1980s* (New York: Bantam Books, 1990), p. 122.

8. Brenner, pp. 69–70.

9. Linn Washington, *Black Judges on Justice: Perspectives from the Bench* (New York: The New Press, 1994), p. 135.

10. Smith, p. 781.

Chapter 5. Benjamin Lawson Hooks

1. Charles Moritz, ed., *Current Biography 1978* (New York: H. W. Wilson Company, 1978), p. 199.

2. Maureen Spizzirri, "Benjamin Hooks, Class of 1948," n.d. <http://www.law.depaul.edu/hooks.html> (March 15, 2001).

3. Ibid.

4. Ibid.

5. Ibid.

6. Barbara Carlisle Bigelow, ed., *Contemporary Black Biography* (Detroit: Gale Research, 1992), p. 110.

7. Lynn Norment, "New Life for an Old Fight," *Ebony*, November 1978, p. 85.

8. Moritz, p. 202.

9. Spizzirri.

Chapter 6. L. Douglas Wilder

1. Laura B. Randolph, "The First Black Elected Governor," *Ebony*, February 1990, p. 24.

2. Ibid., p. 26.

3. Barbara Carlisle Bigelow, ed., *Contemporary Black Biography, Vol. 3* (Detroit: Gale Research, 1993), p. 256.

4. Margaret Edds, *Claiming the Dream: The Victorious Campaign of Douglas Wilder of Virginia* (Chapel Hill, N.C.: Algonquin Books, 1990), p. 34.

5. "Let America Speak: Lawrence Douglas Wilder." n.d. <http://www.pbs.org/williamsburg/voteasvoice/wilder.html> (March 15, 2001).

6. Lawrence Douglas Wilder, "Governor Wilder's Inaugural Address." *Historic Documents of 1990,* Hoyt Gimlin, ed. (Washington, D.C.: Congressional Quarterly Inc., 1991), pp. 46–47.

7. "Former Governor Gives Up Radio Job," Associated Press, March 8, 2001.

8. Leonard R. Colvin, "L. Douglas Wilder—10 Years Later: An Interview with the Nation's First and Only Black Governor," *New Journal and Guide,* January 28, 2000 <http://www.njournalg.com/news/2000/01/douglas_wilder_10years.html> (March 15, 2001).

Chapter 7. Barbara Jordan

1. Barbara Jordan and Shelby Hearon, *Barbara Jordan: A Self-Portrait* (Garden City, N.Y.: Doubleday, 1979), pp. 63–64.

2. Jordan and Hearon, p. 72.

3. Ibid., p. 105.

4. Barbara Carlisle Bigelow, ed., *Contemporary Black Biography, Vol. 4* (Detroit: Gale Research, 1993), p. 139.

5. Jordan and Hearon, pp. 186–187.

6. Barbara Jordan, "Harvard University Commencement Address," June 16, 1977, "Barbara Jordan Quotations," <http://www.rice.edu/armadillo/Texas/Jordan/quotes.html> (March 7, 2001).

Chapter 8. Johnnie Cochran

1. Johnnie Cochran with Tim Rutten, *Journey to Justice* (New York: One World, 1996), p. 10.

2. L. Mpho Mabunda and Shirelle Phelps, eds., *Contemporary Black Biography, Vol. 11*, (Detroit: Gale Research, 1996), pp. 42 43.

3. Cochran, pp. 27–32.

4. Ibid., p 70.

5. Ibid., p. 84.

6. Louise Mooney Collins and Frank V. Castronova, eds., *Newsmakers: The People Behind Today's Headlines, 1996 Cumulation* (Detroit: Gale Research, 1996), p. 99.

7. Ibid., p. 101.

8. Ibid., p. 100.

Chapter 9. Marian Wright Edelman

1. Louise Mooney, ed., *Newsmakers: The People Behind the Headlines, 1990 Cumulation* (Detroit: Gale Research, 1990), p. 118. Citing a *Time* interview.

2. Marian Wright Edelman, *The Measure of Our Success: A Letter to My Children and Yours* (Boston: Beacon, 1992), p. 6.

3. Wallace Terry, "We Don't Have a Child to Waste: An Interview with Marian Wright Edelman," *Parade*, February 14, 1993, p. 5.

4. Barbara Carlisle Bigelow, ed., *Contemporary Black Biography, Vol. 5* (Detroit: Gale Research, 1993), p. 86.

5. Calvin Tomkins, "Profiles: A Sense of Urgency," *The New Yorker*, March 27, 1989, p. 62.

6. "About Us," Children's Defense Fund, n.d. <http://www.childrensdefensefund.org> (March 22, 2001).

7. Tomkins, p. 74.

8. "The State of America's Children Yearbook 2000: 25 Key Facts About American Children," Children's Defense Fund, n.d. <www.childrensdefensefund.org/keyfacts.htm> (March 22, 2001).

9. "Moments in America for Children," Children Defense Fund, n.d. <www.childrensdefensefund.org/factsfigures_moments. htm> (March 22, 2001).

10. "They Cannot Fend for Themselves," *Time*, March 23, 1987, p. 27.

11. "Rev. Jesse L. Jackson, Marian Wright Edelman, Rev. Gardner C. Taylor Awarded Presidential Medal of Freedom," *Jet*, August 28, 2000 <www.findarticles.com> (March 18, 2001).

Chapter 10. Carol Moseley-Braun

1. Jessie Carney Smith, ed., *Notable Black American Women, Book II* (Detroit: Gale Research, 1996), p. 482.

2. Barbara Carlisle Bigelow, ed., *Contemporary Black Biography, Vol. 4* (Detroit: Gale Research, 1993), p. 26.

3. Kathryn A. Haynes, "Campaigning for History: Will Carol Moseley-Braun Be the First Black Woman Senator?" *Ebony*, June 1992, p. 122.

4. Ibid.

5. Bigelow, p. 29.

6. Carol Moseley-Braun, "The Confederate Flag as Racist Symbolism," 138 Congressional Record S9253 (1993); *Rebels in Law: Voices in History of Black Women Lawyers*, J. Clay Smith, Jr., ed. (Ann Arbor, Mich.: University of Michigan Press, 1998), pp. 150–155.

7. Eric L. Smith, "Changing of the Guard: Political Legacy of Former Senator Carol Moseley-Braun," *Black Enterprise*, January 1999 <www.findarticles.com> (March 15, 2001).

8. "Biography: Carol Moseley-Braun, Ambassador to New Zealand and Samoa," U.S. State Department, n.d. <http://www.state.gov/www/about_state/biography/moseley-b_c_newzealand.html> (February 12, 2001).

Further Reading

Cochran, Johnnie, with Tim Rutten. *Journey to Justice.* New York: One World/Ballantine Books, 1996.

Edds, Margaret. *Claiming the Dream: The Victorious Campaign of Douglas Wilder of Virginia.* Chapel Hill, N.C.: Algonquin Books, 1990.

Edelman, Marian Wright. *The Measure of Our Success: A Letter to My Children and Yours.* Boston: Beacon Press, 1992.

Haskins, James. *Thurgood Marshall: A Life for Justice.* New York: Henry Holt and Company, 1992.

Jones, Veda Boyd. *Female Firsts in Their Fields: Government & Politics.* Philadelphia: Chelsea House, 1999.

Jordan, Barbara, and Shelby Hearon. *Barbara Jordan: A Self-Portrait.* Garden City, N.Y.: Doubleday, 1979.

McNeill, Genna Rae. *Groundwork: Charles Hamilton Houston and the Struggle for Civil Rights.* Philadelphia: University of Pennsylvania Press, 1983.

Motley, Constance Baker. *Equal Justice Under Law: An Autobiography.* New York: Farrar, Straus and Giroux, 1998.

Old, Wendie. *Marian Wright Edelman: Fighting for Children's Rights.* Berkeley Heights, N.J.: Enslow Publishers, Inc., 1995.

Ware, Gilbert. *William Hastie: Grace Under Pressure.* New York: Oxford University Press, 1984.

Weatherford, Carole Boston. *The African-American Struggle for Legal Equality in American History.* Berkeley Heights, N.J.: Enslow Publishers, Inc., 2000.

Internet Addresses

Brown v. *Board of Education*, National Archive
   <http://www.archives.gov/digital_classroom/lessons/
   brown_v_board_documents/brown_v_board.html>

Children's Defense Fund
   <http://www.childrensdefense.org>

NAACP Legal Defense and Educational Fund, Inc.,
   Western Regional Office
   <http://www.ldfla.org>

Index